Henry Scott Boys

Some Notes on Java and its Administration by the Dutch

Henry Scott Boys

Some Notes on Java and its Administration by the Dutch

ISBN/EAN: 9783743322417

Manufactured in Europe, USA, Canada, Australia, Japa

Cover: Foto ©ninafisch / pixelio.de

Manufactured and distributed by brebook publishing software (www.brebook.com)

Henry Scott Boys

Some Notes on Java and its Administration by the Dutch

PREFACE.

At Sydney in the spring of 1889 A. D., while I was negotiating a passage to England for my wife and myself *via* China and Japan, an opportunity unexpectedly offered itself of visiting Java *en route* to Hong Kong. We did not let the chance slip, and at once, as became globe trotters, searched the booksellers' shops for anything which might enable us, on reaching the island, to pose before our fellow-travellers as experts in the matter of "Krises" and connoisseurs in coffee. To our disappointment we were unable to find any books of any kind relating to Java, except a record of travel called "The Australian abroad," and we had to content ourselves with the determination to make the best use of our eyes and ears while we were in the island, and to pay an early visit to the British

Museum after our arrival in England to get at the best books which have been written on this most interesting Dutch possession.

From the day when, passing through the straits of Lombok, between the two mighty peaks of Lombok and Bali, we found ourselves within the great volcanic girdle which encircles the Malay Archipelago, until we left Batavia on our way to Singapore, we never ceased to wish that every day which was available might be extended to a month, and that many a friend whom we had left in India could be brought to our side to share in the very thorough enjoyment which our visit to the beautiful region secured for us.

The following pages are the outcome of our short sojourn in Java and of the renewal of the pleasures of that sojourn obtained from what has been written about the island and its administration by the Dutch. Little, except some comparisons between the methods of government adopted by Holland and by the English in the government of their Eastern possessions, and some vain regrets that we, as well as the Dutch, cannot sometimes see ourselves as others see us, can claim in this pamphlet to be original, but I have not shrunk on this account from issuing it, judging that some who have not the time or opportunity to consult the works from which much of my information is drawn, will be glad of that information in a compact form, while I am sure that I myself, on nearing the Javan coast, would have welcomed any such notes on the country I was about to visit.

It is too much to hope that any remarks which I have ventured to make on our administration in Hindustan, or that any description which I have given of the results of a directly contrary system pursued in Java, will have the slightest effect in making our rulers pause and consider whether European methods are in all cases suited to Oriental peoples, and especially whether we are justified in deliberately denationalizing the land. But unquestionably a study of Java and of its government is one of the first duties of an Indian governor, and if that is fairly undertaken it will lead, I think, inevitably to this conclusion, that in many matters it is a mistake to insist that our Oriental subjects should conform to our Western ideas and that, above all, the salvation of the Dutch Government has been its resolute determination to maintain the State's right in the soil, rigidly excluding the middleman and permitting no growth of any proprietary right.

The books which I would suggest to the reader who wishes to further inform himself about Java are—

1. Sir Stamford Raffles' *History of Java*.
2. Sir Stamford Raffles' *Minute on his Administration*.
3. *Java: or, how to manage a Colony*, by J. W. B. Money.
4. *The Malay Archipelago*, by A. R. Wallace.
5. *Max Havalaar*, by Multatuli (E. D. Dekker).

6. *Boro-Boudour, dans l'île de Java*, by Dr. C. Leemans.

7. J. Crawfurd's *History of the Indian Archipelago*, 1820.

8. J. J. Stockdale's *Sketches of Java*, 1812.

9. *Colonial Essays, translated from the Dutch*, by Van der Aa. *Rice and Coffee culture in Java*, 1864.

10. *Official and Secret Papers relating to the Sale of Lands, and other Subjects, during the British Administration of Java*, 1883.

H. S. B.

SOME NOTES ON JAVA.

I.

Although the Dutch have occupied portions of Java for nearly three centuries, they have done but little towards tracing the history or even collecting the traditions of their great dependency; and it was not until after the conquest of the island by the British and its reoccupation by the Dutch in 1814 A.D., that the latter appear to have been awakened to the duty of unravelling, as far as possible, the few clues which were then left to the early history of this most interesting part of what is now called the Malay Archipelago. Without going further back than the commencement of our own era, and probably not further back than some twelve or thirteen centuries, we find that no less than three of the great religions of the world have competed for possession of this beautiful island, and, therefore, as we should expect, the traditions of the people concerning the origin of the races found in the country are broken and confused. But when the Dutch first settled on the shores of Java in 1595 A.D., and when we English a few years afterwards followed to compete with them for its trade, the Mussulmans had not held the government of the country for more than two hundred years, and it is quite certain that, had the early Dutch and English settlers been animated then by the antiquarian spirit, there would have been open to them far more sources of information than are available now or were at hand even when Sir Stamford Raffles, in 1812 A.D., first attempted to glean the few straws which were then left on the field of historical inquiry. Nor have the efforts of the Dutch in the direction of antiquarian research since that date been very systematic or profound; and the successive immigrations of the Hindus, of the races professing and preaching Buddhism, and of the proselytising Mussulmans, still remain shrouded in much uncertainty and offer incomparable attractions to the enthusiastic student of ethnology. Now that a man like Dr. Brandes sits as Curator of the Museum of Antiquities at Batavia, we may hope that the early days of the peoples, who raised such magnificent monuments of devotion as Bram-Banam and Boro

Bodho, will be cleared from much of the mist which at present shuts off the inquirer from any clear view.

The Javan era corresponds within a few years with the Hindu Sambat era, commencing in the year 74 A.D., and it is certain that it is only due to a miscalculation that it does not exactly tally. It is without doubt the same era, and its use by the Javans is absolute proof that the immigrations of the Hindus occurred at a date not prior to the commencement of that cycle. It is not unnatural that the Javans should wish to throw their beginning, as the conquerors of their island, as far back as possible, and we accordingly find them asserting that the founder of the Javan colony arrived from India in the very first year of the era. Aji Saka, who is said to have been prime minister of Prabhu Jaya Bhaya, Prince of Astina, and fifth son of Pandu Devanatta, is named as the leader of the first expedition. He is said to have found the country held by Rasaksas or giants, whom he fought gallantly, but whom apparently he did not subdue, for he returned to his master in Gujerat for reinforcements, with which he succeeded in making good his position in the island.

Other accounts state that the religion and the arts of India were introduced by a Brahman,

Tritesta, at the commencement of the Javan era ; but the fact that the early traditional sovereigns of Java correspond both in order of succession and in name with well-known kings in India, indicates very clearly that the Hindu occupation of the island really commenced after the date of those kings. The accounts, therefore, which put the commencement of the Javan sovereigns five centuries after the first landing of Aji Saka, and which make the first colonisation of the island to have been effected under the sixth descendant of Prabhu Jaya Bhaya of Astina, are certainly more likely to be correct. It is also highly probable that the "Saka" affix to the name Aji only indicates an era, the third Saka of the Kaliyuga, commencing 78 A.D., and that Aji Saka was really only an impersonation of the era itself—an impersonation with which the Hindus in Java subsequently associated the introduction of letters and religion, the framing of their laws and the commencement of settled government. Fa Hian, who visited Java (Ye-pho-ti) in the beginning of the fifth century of our era, says that at that time there were Brahmans and heretics, but no Buddhists on the island. The colonisation must, therefore, have taken place before that date. One fact appears to be quite certain :

the immigration came direct from the continent and not by way of the Malay Peninsula. Java and the contiguous islands of Bali and Madura, which are so near that they may be taken to be a part of Java, abound with the remains of Hindu temples, but in the whole of the Malay Peninsula and in Sumatra there has not been found a sign of Hindu occupation. It is absolutely certain, therefore, that the colonisation of Java was effected by emigrants sailing from India across the Bay of Bengal. The accounts which attribute the foundation of the first permanent settlement to the sixth descendant of Prabhu Jaya Bhaya tell that he sailed with 5,000 followers in six large ships and first landed in Sumatra, but, not finding the country agree with that which had been described by Aji Saka, he re-embarked and finally reached the land of promise, settling at Matarem and being proclaimed under the name of Sawela Chala. Two thousand more emigrants with their wives and families followed soon after, and a city was founded, called Mendang Kamulan, afterwards named Bram-Banam, the date of this event being given as 525 Javan era, or 603 A.D. Other accounts make Prabhu Jaya Bhaya himself to have reigned in Java in the year 1000, Javan era, and Bram-Banam to have been founded eighteen years afterwards The earlier date would seem to be the most probable.

The remains of the temples at **Bram**-Banam attest the size and importance **of Mendang** Kamulan, and of the principality **of which it** was the capital. **So numerous** are the smaller temples which **surround the** central edifice that **the place** is spoken **of as** the "thousand **temples," and in actual numbers there** still **exist** between **two and three hundred.** The extraordinary feature **of this group of buildings** is that, while the central **pile was undoubtedly** Brahmanical—containing **as** it does **an image of** Durga, which might have **been** brought **from** any of Kali's shrines in India, so exact is the **reproduction of the goddess in the** act of destroying—**and while many of the statues** which are found around the **place are also Brahmanical,** the smaller surrounding temples contain each **a** most unmistakable figure of Buddha, **similar to** those **found** on the great Stupa of Boro Bodho, which is **a** pure Buddhist monument without the faintest admixture of Brahmanism. This very remarkable mingling of the two re**ligions is** characteristic **of a very** large number of the sacred buildings of Java, and it clearly indicates that for many generations the two faiths existed side by side, the adherents of each agreeing to live amicably one with the other, and probably each adopting portions of the worship of the other's religion. Indeed, this fair land of Java seems to have set an example to the Eastern world of toleration, for when, centuries after, the Mussulmans succeeded in converting the whole population to the religion of Mahomed, the proselytising was not effected, as in other Oriental countries, with fire and sword : and the perfect state in which we find such edifices as Boro Bodho show that there was in the process no exhibition of that iconoclastic zeal which usually has distinguished the propagation of Islam. This is especially fortunate in a land like Java, where there exist but few trustworthy written records, and where history will largely have to be read in the stones of her monuments.

A most remarkable fact about the few records which do exist is the entire absence of any mention of the Buddhists. We have apparently absolutely no tradition of the introduction of the law, no account of the arrival of any missionaries, no history of any contest between the rituals or the dogmas of the two religions. This doubtless is largely accounted for by the friendly terms, if not terms of partnership, on which the Brahmans and the Order had mutually agreed to live. Had the two religions been in open conflict one with the other we should most undoubtedly have heard much in the histories, however incomplete and untrustworthy in other respects, of the tyranny or the hateful tenets of the respective sects. Silence on these points on the part of the historians clearly indicates that they saw nothing abnormal in the relations of the two religions, and that those relations were amicable and had lasted for some generations prior, at any rate, to the writings of the annals. Dr. Leemans in his elaborate monograph on the Stupa of Boro Bodho says that in the sixth century of the Christian era we find Buddhism and Brahmanism existing in Java side by side, that in the ninth century Buddhism had taken the lead, and that in the twelfth or thirteenth it began to yield to Sivaism : but he does not detail his ground for making these statements. Apparently Dr. Friederich had discovered some inscriptions, which, however, have not been published. One fact about Buddhism in Java is certain. It was not imported from Southern India, either with the original emigrants or at a subsequent date, nor was it imported from Ceylon or Burma. The Buddhism of these countries was that of the Southern Church, while all the Buddhist remains in Java tell us plainly that the tenets and the ritual of the Northern Church ruled in that island. The Northern Church occupied Nepal, Tibet and China, so that we are led to the conclusion that the preaching of the law in Java was possibly done by Chinese missionaries, and the first intercourse with China is said to have occurred in the time of Panji, an adventurer, who obtained considerable power about the tenth Javan century. We may perhaps then assume, in want of better grounds, that the Javans made their first acquaintance with the purer religion about 1000, Javan era. It is generally thought that the Stupa at Boro Bodho was constructed about 1200 (Javan): and the wonderful preservation of the fabric would certainly indicate that its date cannot be very much more ancient. On the other hand the Buddhism of the builder of Boro Bodho was of a very pure type, and could scarcely have come from China at a very late date.

If Buddhism was introduced from China, then, curiously enough, the first contact of the Javans with Islam occurred about the same time, the son of Kuda Lalean, a Javan sovereign, having visited India about 1084 (Javan), where he became a convert to Mahomedanism. It was, however, not until nearly three centuries later that Mahomedanism became a prominent religion in the country. In 1247 (Javan) Raden Wijaya established the great kingdom of Majapahit, the rulers of which extended their sovereignty over the whole island, and also exercised a protectorate over Sumatra. This was the last great Hindu Raj which held sway in Java, and the remnants of the Brahmans, who still exist in Bali, look back with longing and regret to those last days of their glory. On the northern coast of Java Islam was gradually obtaining a firm hold, conversion to the new faith being the work of Arab missionaries who came from the rich shores of the islands of the Archipelago. By the middle of the fourteenth (Javan) century there were several centres of aspiring Mahomedans, and in 1400 (Javan) these Mussulmans, conspiring with certain base-born sons of the Majapahit Raja, overthrew the Hindu dynasty with its Prince Augka Wijaya, destroyed the city and set up a Mahomedan kingdom with its capital at Demak. By 1421 the whole island, with the exception of the westernmost principalities, had become Mahomedan. The Hindus, who resisted conversion, fled to Bali, an island at the extreme south-eastern extremity of Java, and thither the Mussulmans have never followed them.

SOME NOTES ON JAVA.

When the Portuguese first visited Java in 1511 A. D. they found a Hindu king still reigning in Bantam, but within the sixteenth century of our era this principality also had submitted to the new religion.

It is clear, however, that Mahomedanism has never sunk into the souls of the Javans as it has in other Oriental countries, and a Wahabi, and even an average Mussulman of India, would be scandalised at the want of zeal on the part of these simple sons of Islam. To the Anglo-Indian travelling through the country it is scarcely apparent that there is a single Mahomedan in it. No mosques or idgahs are visible, no muezzin is heard, no devout Moslem is noticed by the wayside or at the house-door falling on his knees at the hour of prayer. In the families of the well-to-do classes the ceremonies attending the peculiar rite by which children are admitted to Islam, include processions, accompanied with much display, through the streets, but no stranger would imagine that the spectacle was a part of a Mahomedan rite. Fabulous beasts of all kinds, giants and giantesses, trophies such as might appear in a Lord Mayor's show, follow one another in quick succession, but no sign of the faith of Mahomed is to be seen. The whole thing is clearly a survival of the old Hindu pageants which have been adapted to the new ceremonies. When our sepoys during our occupation in 1812—14 A. D. celebrated the Mohurram after Indian fashion, they very much astonished the Javans. The only bigoted religionists are the Hadjis, almost without exception Arabs, who figure as Moulvis or panghulus (village priests) and who take care to drive a good trade in tithes and fees. These Hadjis are invariably found to be at the bottom of all the insurrections with which the Dutch have had to deal. The Dutch in consequence discourage as much as possible all pilgrimages to Mecca, as they find the lower Hadjis are apt to make common cause with the foreign Sheikh.

II.

It was in 1595 A. D. that the Dutch first appeared in Java and established their settlement at Bantam, in the west of the island. Thence they proceeded along the coast to Madura at the far eastern extremity, and here they were guilty of a barbarous massacre of the inhabitants. In 1598 A. D. they returned to Bantam, and not long afterwards obtained a position on the swamps of Jakatra, where in 1621 A. D. they founded their town of Batavia. After the fall of Majapahit in 1478 A. D. the island of Java had broken up into a number of petty states once more, which for the next century and a-half, time after time, were united into larger kingdoms, only once again and again to suffer disruption. The Dutch availed themselves of these internecine quarrels to advance their own interests, and in 1646 A. D. they negotiated their first treaty. This was followed by other treaties, ranging from 1677 A. D. to 1691 A. D., securing the cession of large territory and monopolies of pepper, sugar and cloths. The English during this period had been at Bantam, where they settled in 1602 A. D., but in 1683 A. D. they retired from the competition with the Dutch and withdrew from Java altogether just as Holland obtained control over the whole island, with the exception of the Sultanates of Surakarta and Jokhyokarta in the east and the Preanger territories in the south-west. In the middle of the eighteenth century the Dutch were engaged in a prolonged war with the object of subduing the eastern portion of the island. Up to 1742 A. D. the whole of this portion of Java was held by the Susuhnan. The Dutch, taking advantage of the ambition of a young prince of the reigning family, by name Manhu Buni, urged him privately to lay claim to the province of Matarem as his appanage, a province which the Dutch wished to detach from the Susuhnan. Manhu Buni, nothing loth, made his claim, which was, as calculated by the Dutch, scornfully rejected. A civil war was commenced, which gave the Dutch the opportunity they wanted, and, after twelve years, they succeeded in partitioning the dominions of the Susuhnan into three portions. One, now called the Sultanat of Surakarta, sixteen districts, remained with the Susuhnan; another, seven districts, went to Manhu Buni as Sultan of Jokhyokarta, and the third portion, thirty districts, by far the largest slice of the whole, embracing a stretch of 250 miles of coast line, was ceded to **the Dutch, by** whom it has been ever since held. The Sultans after the issue of **this** war held their reduced dominions as vassals of the **Dutch**, until, in the third decade of the present century, a second war left the Princes with practically nothing left of their old territories except their private domains. During the eighteenth cen**tury** the Dutch Indies were administered by the Dutch East India Company, their charter including Sumatra and many of the islands in the Archipelago. This century of maladministration landed the Company in **1795 A. D. in** debt to the amount of 160 **millions of florins, or** 13 millions sterling.

The **Company** was dissolved and a Commission was appointed from Holland, which merely suggested reductions and failed to cut away the root of the evil, which was the monopoly system. The deficits still went on, **and** then attention was turned towards the methods pursued in British India. Ignorance, however, of these institutions, combined with prejudice in favour of exclusive trading, defeated amendment, and another Commission, which sat in 1803 A. D., maintained the forced contingents of produce, the forced services and the monopolies of pepper and coffee. Certain reforms in the judicial and the police administration were recommended, as also were the separation of the Government proper from the direction of trade, which was to be handed over to a Board of Revenue and Commerce. The resolution on this report abolished monopolies: but it fell through, and Marshall Daendels was sent out to institute reforms and protect the natives. He did nothing, says Raffles, but squeeze them a little tighter. In 1811 A. D. Holland became a province of France and the English at once occupied Java, which they held for three years, restoring the island to the Dutch in 1814 A. D.

The occupation of Java by the English seems to be a convenient point in its history at which to take a brief survey of the country in its economic, social and political aspects as they presented themselves to an observer at that time, and as they are described by Sir Stamford Raffles in his graphic account of Java and the Javans in his Minutes, written as Governor-General of this island and of the other islands of the Archipelago. The island of Java measures 666 miles in length, varying in breadth from 135 to 56 miles, and is 50,000 square miles in area. It forms the western end of that belt of volcanic islands which encircles the Malay Archipelago, and which is traceable through Bali,

SOME NOTES ON JAVA.

Lombok, Sombawa, Flores, and Timor. From one end to the other it is mountainous, there being few plains which are unbroken for many miles by one range or another. All these ranges **are** volcanic, and the number of volcanoes are innumerable, over forty of them being more or less active at the present day. Semeru, the loftiest, is 12,238 feet high. The eruptions of some of them have been very terrible within the memory of living Javans, the latest being that of Krakatoa, an island lying in the Straits of Sumatra. In the eastern part of the island is a singular crater, that of Grobogan, more than a mile across, the greater portion of the **area of** which is covered with a crust of caked volcanic earth, while in the centre is a large lake of boiling mud, similar to, but much vaster than, Tikitiri in New Zealand, from which great globes of mud rise almost free of the hideous cauldron and fall back with appalling throbs into the seething mass, only to be forced up again and again by the power of the steam below. In 1822 the outburst from Galung-gung destroyed 114 villages and 4,000 lives were lost. Another eruption in 1867 killed 1,000 people in the district of Jokhyokarta, and in 1872 the eruption of Merapi was very severe. **Off** Banjuwangi submarine earthquakes are very frequent, and twice, within a very few years, both the ocean telegraph cables between Java **and** Australia have been destroyed at a point not many miles distant from the eastern extremity of Java.

The soil of the valleys is extraordinarily fertile, consisting entirely of the disintegrated *débris* of the mountains and continually renewed year by year by the washings from the hill sides. The eastern end of the island is more fertile than the western : **and** yet the western is magnificent, even when it is compared with the richest plains of Hindustan. It may be said, indeed, that the soil is absolutely inexhaustible everywhere. No manure is ever given nor is any required, for the water, which **is trained on** to the cultivated lands from the sides of the mountain by the most elaborate system of irrigation ducts, brings its own manure with it in the shape of the most fertilising pulverised volcanic soil. The teak forests are very fine, occupying at the present time, it is estimated, some 2,300 square miles. The denudation of this magnificent timber land has been proceeding almost as recklessly as in our Australian Colonies, but fortunately the continuous moisture of the undergrowth checks damage by forest fires.

The hills not only ensure fertility to the valleys, but they furnish every climate short of the Sub-Arctic. The volcanic peak of Bali is 11,000 feet high, and throughout the island these magnificent cones, each like a Vesuvius, but ten times larger, rise into the sky, springing themselves from uplands which are elevated from three to five thousand feet above the **sea.** The result is that, though the island is so near the Equator, the climate of many places is quite temperate, and in those parts is exceedingly healthy and suitable for Europeans. So much is this the case that in 1672 A. D., when Holland was overrun by the French under Louis XIV., the Dutch actually contemplated transferring the whole of the population *en masse* to Java. In the low grounds near the coast the Hollanders would have plenty of opportunity of introducing the familiar canals of the home **country,** and this they have actually done **in all the principal** seaport towns, such as Batavia, Samarang and Soerabia, with, however, very doubtful advantage, for the malaria in these cities is **very** bad, and it cannot be lessened by these canals, which are cut through the inhabited quarters in many directions.

The wet season lasts from October to April. There is incessant thunder and lightning, but the storms are not violent and the seas of this part of the Archipelago are almost always smooth and quiet. These waters are therefore well suited to the native form of boat, the "prahu," in which the Javans boldly venture out fishing fifty or sixty miles from land, absolutely certain of getting a steady breeze in the latter part of the day to bring them landwards. The Javans never seem to have advanced in ship-building beyond the "prahu," which is an open boat; and this indicates that all external commerce must have been carried on by other nations seeking Java, such as the Malays, Bugis (of the Celebes), Indians, Chinese, and Arabs. The Javans themselves never ventured beyond their own coasts and the islands in the immediate vicinity in the search of trade. Descended, as most of them must be, from the daring mariners who crossed the Bay of Bengal in search of new lands, it seems strange that this should have been the case. Java was in former times the granary of the eastern islands, and in addition to rice she exported in Raffles' time, for the use of the other Malay islands, salt, oil, tobacco, timber, Java cloths, brassware, &c., while she imported from the same islands tin from Banka, Bugi cloth from the Celebes, ponies from Sumbawa, gold dust, diamonds, camphor, tortoise-shell, **dyeing** woods, nutmegs, cloves, mace, beche de mer and edible birds'-nests. These last mentioned articles of commerce **sold in** Raffles' time for their weight in silver, the Chinese being the buyers. Java, as well as other islands in the Archipelago, produces these, **and** Holland used to **get a** revenue **of** 200,000 dollars per annum **from** this item alone. The bird which constructs **this** nest is a swallow which builds in the caverns in the rocks. The nests are gathered sometimes twice a year, just after the young are fledged, but care must be taken **not to drive** away the birds by too frequent disturbance.

The ancient Javan commerce was all but annihilated **by** the Dutch restrictive system, native traders being forbidden to traffic in any of the articles included in the Dutch monopolies, *e.g.*, coffee, salt, indigo, opium, timber, **four** kinds of spices, pepper, **tin, Surat silks, Indian** cloths and Japan copper, while numerous prohibitory **orders were** issued about navigation to and **from** certain ports, shackling every movement of commerce. **The ordinances obstructed** trade in the interior quite as much as on the sea and at the **ports, endless** transit dues being levied on all merchandise **at every** stage. These transit **dues were farmed out** to the

Chinese, who levied pretty well what they pleased, and into whose hands the unrestricted trade of the country, except the local bazaar trade, naturally passed.

Marshall Daendels constructed with forced labour a magnificent grand Trunk Road from one end of the island to the other, and cross roads of a similar kind were made leading to the main ports; but the natives were not allowed to use these metalled lines of communication. They were compelled to follow their own tracks. Nothing strikes the traveller so much, even at the present day, as the perfect state in which these military lines of communication are kept: the very sides of the road looking as if they were swept and sodded, the grass banks topped with neat bamboo fencing and each tree protected while young with the same kind of trellis-work. All this is effected at a nominal cost to the Government, the whole being carried out by the Corvée system. But no less remarkable is the entire absence of cart traffic on these lines. It is evidently still forbidden. Pack animals alone are allowed. The system of post travelling is as well arranged as the roads are good. At every five miles a covered archway spans the road, under which on each side are stabled the Government stage ponies. The traveller's hired **carriage, generally a** small phaeton, **draws up** under this staging house, out of the sun and sheltered from rain; the six ponies, which are **the ordinary team,** are changed, and away speeds the traveller over the well-kept track. The fares for these journeys are not high, and **the stranger is** inclined to think much good **of a Government** which looks after his comfort so successfully.

III.

As we are swiftly and pleasantly carried through the Javan uplands in our well-found stage carriage, drinking in the soft morning air of an April day, we can follow up at our leisure the thoughts suggested by the scenes we pass through and the faces we meet on the wayside. Life in the country in Java is astir very early in the day. With the dawn the roads begin to look like ant-tracks, so thickly are they thronged with the peasantry on their way to the fields or the bazaar. For the markets are held at sunrise and all such business is concluded early in the day. The village markets look like what are sometimes seen in India—"meena bazaars:" for not a male creature is to be seen in them. Buyers and sellers are one and all women, and very practical dealers they seem, doing their business without one-fifth of the noise which rises from an Indian bazaar. All the village women dress in one unvarying colour— indigo blue—wearing nothing on their heads, their hair drawn off the face and knotted at the back of the head. Their clothes are universally neat and good of their kind. The cloth is all woven in the peasants' own houses, each house containing a spinning wheel and a loom. Scarcely a man, woman or child is to be seen in rags. The women wear the *sarong*, a cloth joined at the ends and wrapped round the waist and legs as a petticoat. Round the body, supporting the breasts, is wrapped a cloth called the *kemban*, and over all is worn a loose chemise or gown (*kalambi*) reaching to the knees. The ladies in the upper classes wear coloured sarongs of bright red and yellow patterns, the manufacture of which sometimes is very costly, the process of getting out the pattern with the aid of wax and the dyeing tub involving much time and labour. Over the body is worn a white jacket (*kobaia*), and on the feet which are bare the smartest of slippers. *Voila tout!* The Dutch ladies most sensibly have adopted this dress, and up to five o'clock in the afternoon they wear nothing else, walking out, driving and doing their shopping in this costume, supplemented by a smart sunshade. The native men of the lower orders wear drawers, the sarong (unjoined and called a *jarit*) folded round the waist, a jacket with short sleeves and a handkerchief on the head, worn turban fashion. Often to this is added an enormous spreading hat made of leaves or of bamboo, and still more often a hat which looks like an inverted basin, in which the head half disappears and which is coloured outside with gold, red and blue patterns. Neither men nor women cut their hair. The former gather it into a knot on the top of the head, as the women do at the back.

The pan-dan must have been imported from India by those who came from there in the first settlements, and pan-eating is as much a habit as in India. Other favourite delicacies are not so unobjectionable, especially *trasi* or *blachang*, which are dried shrimps, salted and pounded into cheeses. The putrescent fluid from these is made into a sauce, and the intolerable stench which loads the air as a consignment of this truly awful concoction goes by on its way up from the coast is indescribable. Some Javans still refuse to eat cow's or bullock's flesh, retaining their Hindu prejudices. Neither will they eat any milk food, butter or cheese—the idea being doubtless the same as the reason which induced Manu to forbid the flesh of cattle, namely, the protection of agricultural stock. A Javan again points to his Hindu descent when he refuses to use his left hand at his dinner. The meals are served exactly as in Hindustan, the diners sitting on the ground, cross-legged, and the meals being served on brass or wooden dishes. The staple food is of course rice. But of whatever the dinner may consist, all certainly get enough and are well fed. This fact is well marked. The children especially show signs of care and good nourishment. Their sturdy little limbs and quick movements are very pleasant to watch. No such miserable little scarecrows are to be seen as are only too common in villages in British India.

The villages and the houses in them match their owners. There is no crowding of hut against hut, as in India, where the pressure of population or other causes have compressed the village dwellings into as small space as possible. In Java it is not unusual for the inhabited portion of the village to occupy at least one-tenth of the whole area, and when we penetrate the neat trellis work fence which surrounds the "campong" we find that each cultivator's hut has an enclosure with a small garden, the bamboo being again brought into requisition to make a surrounding fence, with an ornamental lych gate at the entrance. The houses have no mud walls. They are made entirely of wood, bamboo, wattle and thatch. Flowers and creepers are not wanting and the signs of comfort and prosperity are conspicuous. The open "alum-alum" (or "chaupal") is kept clean and trim: and on one side is the unpretentious mosque, a structure of bamboo and leaves, and opposite to it the house of **the bakal, or, as** he would be styled in Hindustan, lumberdar or patel. In the middle of the alum-alum grows the familiar fig tree, and as we gaze we admire the tenacity with which the Hindu clung to the **remembrance of** his old home when he was **transplanted into this new** country. Looking from a hillside down upon a plain studded with these picturesque villages, each embowered in a luxuriant growth of bamboos and **trees, the** spectator is reminded much of some of the **lovely "duns"** on the road into Kashmir, short of **the** Rattan Pir. The hamlets look like green **islets in a sea** of golden rice.

Immediately outside the ring fence which has been described commences the **rice or other** cultivation. Not a square yard of ground seems to be wasted, and the care and evident labour **with which each** bit of slope is terraced and supported, **the greatest** area thus being obtained for the rice crop, **is most** admirable. These terraces are carried up **the** sides of the highest **mou**ntains, the mighty volcanoes themselves allowing the cultivation **to creep up** within what **loo**ks a dangerous distance from their craters. The water for irrigating the crops is brought from the hillsides and is unfailing. This enables the cultivator to get two rice crops off the same field, and this staple appears on the village lands in the month of April, in all stages of growth from sowing to harvest. The main crops are rice, Indian corn, beans, sugarcane (eight kinds), coffee, pepper, indigo and tobacco. During the past three years a blight has affected the sugarcane, stunting the growth and seriously diminishing the outturn. This has been a severe blow to the factories. Rice is still an article of export, so that, in spite of the enormous increase of the population, which now is said to reach twenty millions as against five millions in Raffles' time, the island more than feeds itself. The cocoa tree, with its beautiful blossoms and fruit, both on the tree at the same time, is to be found in many of the peasants' gardens, and the cocoanut and the sugar palms abound. All the Indian fruits are to be seen in the bazaars, together with the dorian and the mangosteen.

Wayside stalls for refreshment are numerous, those for cooling drinks, apparently mostly concocted with rice water, being especially noticeable. But the "kalwar," with his tempting array of dirty bottles, is conspicuously absent. Not a liquor shop is to be seen, and it is a fact that the people are eminently temperate. No doubt the Mahomedan religion has much to say to this, and such drinking as goes on is done in private. The Dutch, however, discourage all liquor traffic, and the use of opium is much restricted. The upper classes, corrupted by luxury, just as in British India, indulge in drinking far more than the lower orders, as they also excel them in other forms of vice and sensuality. Those who smoke—and the habit is certainly not so prevalent as in Hindustan—smoke cigarettes, the tobacco being rolled up in the thin dry leaf that is stripped off the head of the Indian corn. Chewing or sucking tobacco is the commoner mode of enjoying the weed among the vulgar, and the sight of a twist of shag tobacco stuck between the front teeth and the lips, protruding out of the mouth and obstructing all speech, is not pleasant to look upon.

As the Anglo-Indian passes through the outskirts of the villages he is not surprised to see going on the very same competition in kite-flying which is so familiar in Hindustan. This with cock-fighting, quail-fighting, pigeon-flying and also, among those who can afford such spectacles, animal fights, such as tiger *versus* buffalo, bull *versus* bull, and ram *versus* pig, are clearly survivals of Hindu customs brought with them by the emigrants. Not so with their music and musical instruments. Fortunately the original Indian colonists left behind their tomtoms and their other instruments of ear-torture. Neither in the Javan airs nor in the character of their orchestra is there any trace to be found of the music of Hindustan. The immigrant Hindus have got their scales, their melodies and their instruments from the aborigines or from the neighbouring islands. The *gamlan pelog*, or full band, consists mainly of large metal or wooden harmonicas struck in slow cadence, blows on metal gongs of varying depth of sound marking the pauses. There is also a harp which plays a subordinate part and a drum which is unobtrusive. There are no stringed instruments other than the harp, and there are no wind instruments. The airs are in the major key and the effect is exceedingly good. A complete "gamlan" costs from 3,000 to 4,000 florins.

The national dance is almost the exact reproduction of the Indian nautch, and the nautch girls also correspond both in appearance and in their mode of life. The drama of the country consists of shadow plays, shadows being cast **upon a screen** with the **aid** of puppets. The plots are taken from the Hindu mythology, the wars of the Pandus and the story **of** Rama. Scenes **from** the earlier history **of Java are** also enacted, and a careful study **of these shadow** plays would probably throw some light on the first days of the Hindu occupation.

While the surroundings and the amusements of Javan peasantry are under notice, it will not be out of place to quote more or less fully **Sir Stamford Raffles' opinion of the** Javan character. When he inquired of the Dutch their character he found them stigmatised as indolent, treacherous and deceitful. Sir Stamford admits that among the higher orders were to be found **in** many cases violence, deceit and gross sensuality, but he considers **the Javan** peasants to be simple, **natural and ingenuous.** He found them generous and warm-hearted ; **in their** domestic relations kind, affectionate, gentle and **contented ;** in their public relations obedient, **honest and** faithful. In their intercourse with society this keen observer saw them display in a high degree the virtues of honesty, plain deal**ing** and candour. Prisoners brought to the bar in nine cases out of ten, he found, confessed without disguise or equivocation the full extent and exact circumstances of their offences, and communicated, when required, more information on the matter at issue than all the rest of the evidence, reminding us forcibly of the ordinary Indian offender.

They seemed to be liberal and profuse where this was possible, and fond of show and display, while they undoubtedly were most hospitable. He found them most keenly sensitive to praise or shame, but he thought that either national oppression or their agricultural habits had rendered them somewhat indifferent to military glory. They were characterised rather by passive fortitude than by active courage, and endured privations with patience. While mostly strangers to unrelenting hatred, jealousy would urge them to serious crime, and a husband's wounded honour would be seldom healed. In manners they were easy, courteous and respectful even to timidity, while in every family the respect for parents and old age was most marked. A strong corroboration of the truth of this picture of the Javan peasant's character is found in the fact that the description might be applied word for word to the Indian ryot, where he can be found living his own simple life, undemoralised by strife in the law courts or struggles with an oppressive landlord.

Raffles says that when the English took possession of the country they found that the Dutch invariably slept with closed **doors** and guarded houses, but that the English kept their houses open night and day, and their confidence was not misplaced. But it must be remembered that this remark was made in 1811 A. D., just after the terribly vigorous administration of Marshal Daendels. That **officer, as** we have seen, was sent to Java "to protect the natives." This shows that, in the opinion of Holland, the people had not altogether been well treated, but Marshal Daendel's idea of protection was to sacrifice 10,000 lives in the construction of his system of military roads, and under his administration many districts were nearly depopulated by the migrations from the Dutch Provinces to the Native **States. Un**der this state of things it is not wonderful that the Dutch slept uneasy in their beds, or that they pronounced the Javans to be deceitful and treacherous.

The Javans **proper are an** agricultural race, closely attached to the soil, of quiet habits and contented disposition. They leave trade almost entirely to the Malays and Bujis, **who** being maritime and commercial races, are adventur‐ **ous and ac**customed **to** distant and hazardous enterprises. These people are found mostly in the seaports and generally have their own *quartiers* in the cities. The trade in the interior is almost entirely in the hands of the Chinese, of whom, in Raffles' time, there were 100,000 in the island : and the mixed race between these people and the Javans is also very numerous. Prior to the English occupation the settled policy of the Dutch had been to depress the natives and encourage the Chinese, whom they found to be exceedingly useful as farmers of the revenue. A reaction from this policy has now set in and immigration from China is discouraged. It is possibly the great superiority of the soil which accounts for the tenacity with which the Javan clings to his agricultural pursuits ; it is more probable that the characteristics of the Indian race are reproduced in the Javan. Again, as in India, "infancy and marriage go together," the husband of sixteen taking home his bride of thirteen. Marriage contracts are almost identical in their steps with Hindu usage. A bachelor is well nigh unknown. If the bridegroom cannot attend the marriage ceremony he sends his "kris" as proxy ! Dissolutions of marriage are frequent and easily obtained, the wife paying a fine and the husband giving alimony :

but children cost little to rear and are valuable for their services. They therefore do not suffer from this cause.

Slavery, up to Raffles' time, had been promoted by the Dutch, and he estimated that there were 30,000 slaves in the island. No Javan was, however, ever reduced to slavery, this class being entirely recruited from the neighbouring islands. It is probable that the connection formed with the indigenous Javans by the conquering colonists saved the whole native-born population from liability to slavery after the settlement of the country. It seems, however, that the condition of slaves in Java was never intolerable. It is possible that the system of forced labour—which is, and apparently always has been, such a marked feature in the economics of Java—may have been a survival of the servile labour of the indigenous Javanese, but it is more likely that in this, as in so many other customs, the Indian principle was introduced and "begari" became an important element in the social Javan life. No Javan thinks of disputing the claim of his chief to dispose of a large portion of his labour just as he pleases, and the labour is given just as much as a matter of course to the Government, when it is required. As may be expected, this system works in many cases terribly unequally and oppressively, but its effects will be considered more conveniently when the land tenures are discussed.

The labour of women in the country districts is as much valued as that of the men. The men plough, harrow and weed: the women transplant, reap and carry. In the fields agriculturists are entirely relieved from one portion of labour which falls so heavily on our cultivators in India. No water has to be raised. Abundance of irrigation is obtained from the hundreds of channels which run all over the country, and no machinery of any kind is required to bring water to each man's field. Curiously enough, up to Raffles' time the Javans themselves used no mill for expressing the juice from the sugarcane, but left this process to the Chinese, obtaining their sugar entirely from the tari tree. All this has been changed, and there is now, under the culture system (of which more hereafter), an enormous area under cane.

In the matter of education the Dutch adopted, and still to this day adopt, a very decided policy. They deliberately keep the Javans ignorant of all Western literature. There are schools in the villages, generally presided over by one of the priests, but instruction in Dutch or in any other language except the Javan vernacular is rigorously excluded. Primary education alone is attended to, **and no** higher education of any kind permitted. Neither **is** the use of Dutch in conversation with natives encouraged: and should a Javan acquainted with the Dutch colloquial address an official in that language he finds himself at once checked and rebuked by being answered in the vernacular. The Hollanders at any rate are determined that they will create for themselves no difficulties of the sort that they see surrounding the English in India. They argue that the Javans would generally make no good use of their education, and the spectacle of the "Congress" certainly leads **them to think** that this opinion **is well justified. This is only** one of the points in which the Dutch system is diametrically opposite to the liberal and self-sacrificing policy of the British, and it is this contrast **in** the administration which makes the study of the **government by** Holland of its great Oriental dependency and a consideration of the results so intensely interesting and instructive to the Anglo-Indian.

The **Javan** language **is** no doubt the language **of** the aborigines, or rather of the race which occupied the island when it was colonised by the Hindus, largely mingled with words of Sanscrit origin. Valentyne says that in the high or court Javan language at least three out of four words come direct from the Sanskrit: and this is exactly what we should have expected, the Hindus as conquerors insisting on imposing their tongue upon the conquered race, just as the Norman haughtily disdained to accept Saxon from those whom he had subdued. The consequence is that there still run side by side two Javan vernaculars—the polite language in which Hindu words abound, and the language of the commons in which they are far less frequent. Both languages, however, are written in the same character, which is a corrupt form of the Pali: and this indicates that the aborigines possessed no written characters until the Hindus introduced theirs into the island. Nor have any such characters been found on any inscriptions. The language of the common people owes little or nothing to the Arabic, in spite of the intercourse with the Malays. It has four very distinct dialects, the Sunda in the west and south-west, the Javan in the north and east, and the dialects of Madura and Bali. In this vulgar tongue nouns have no gender, number, or case, and adjectives are indeclinable. In addressing one of the upper classes a Javan is obliged to use the court language, and similarly children in addressing their parents will, as far as possible, use the same language in token of respect. The people, therefore, have really to be acquainted with both vernaculars. The classic language "Kawi," in which nearly all mythological poems are written, consists almost entirely of Sanskrit, and this in a far less corrupted form than the Pali. In Bali, which is the last stronghold of Hinduism, the Kawi is still the language of religion and of law, the knowledge of it being mainly confined to the Brahmans. The Kawi was undoubtedly the channel through which the Sanskrit element penetrated the vernacular dialects of Java, and even now the educated and half-educated will endeavour to introduce Kawi words into their writings, just as the police diary writer in India interlards his jargon with Persian and Arabic words. Devanagri is also found in some few manuscripts, and there are inscriptions in this character on some of the temples. All old writings of importance, such as the mythological works mentioned above, are in verse, and we find the origin of the Hindu deities, the wars of the Pandus, &c., all localised. In the Ramayana, however, the story is for the main part laid in India, and is only so far localised that, after the death of Ravana, Hanuman is made to migrate to Java. The custom of burying dates in sentences by giving certain values to words and letters obtains as in Persia and India.

IV.

The land system, obtaining in Java when the Dutch first landed, was almost identical with that prevailing in Hindustan, and it is quite certain that it was carried from the latter country to their new settlements by the emigrant Hindus. We find the sovereign acknowledged without question as the owner of the soil, the cultivator occupying it under unvarying conditions, the governors receiving assignments of the revenue of large areas in payment for their services in administration. Proprietary right, as we English understand it, never existed. The land was national property, the nation being represented by the sovereign. Sir Stamford Raffles, after a very full investigation into the land-tenures, writes:—"Generally speaking, no proprietary right in the soil is vested in anyone between the cultivator and sovereign, the intermediate classes, who may at any time have enjoyed the revenues of villages or districts, being deemed the executive officers of Government who received these revenues as a gift from their lord, and who depended on his will alone for their tenure." Again, Herr Knops, one of the Dutch Commissioners for the investigation of land-tenures, writes:—"There is not a single Javan who supposes that the soil is the property of the regent, but they are all sensible that it belongs to the Government, nominally called the sovereign among them. The Javan's idea of property is modified by the three kinds of subjects to which it is applied: rice-fields, gagas, or fruit trees. A Javan has no rice-field he can call his own. Those of which he had the use of last year will be exchanged next year for others. They circulate from one cultivator to another, and if any villager were excluded, he would infallibly emigrate. It is different with the gagas, or lands where dry rice is cultivated. The cultivator who clears such lands from trees or brushwood and reclaims them from a wilderness, considers himself to be a proprietor of the same. With regard to fruit trees, the Javan cultivator claims those he has planted as his legal property without any impost. If a chief were to transgress against this right the village would be deserted."

No co-parcenary communities are traceable anywhere in the island, indicating that no collector of revenue or headman of a village has ever yet succeeded in so strengthening his position as to become actually the proprietor, capable of leaving the property to his heirs. The boundaries of villages in Java are not well defined as in India—a fact which indicates the absence of all idea of property either on the part of an individual landlord or of a community. No sales of land have been known, although the assignees of the revenue could sell their assignments to others. This system of "pusakas," or jaghirs, as they would be called in India, was carried to a great length. Every "tumangung" or ruler of a province was paid by the sovereign by a pusaka. He in his turn would grant pusakas to his demangs (tehsildars), and the demang to the bukal (lambardar). Similarly all the underlings and petty officials, the kliwons, the jeyang-sekars (armed police), the retinues of the chiefs of various grades,—all were paid in assignments of the revenues of lands. All this opened the door to great abuses, but in no cases did the grantees succeed in usurping the proprietary right. No length of holding, no application of industry or capital could justify any Javan in calling any rice-grounds his own. Nor could he gain a title even to a definite term of occupancy. Nor, ofcourse, could any right of inheritance accrue. As a matter of convenience the cultivators' heirs succeeded to their fathers' position, just as the son of the bukal might succeed his father in the headship of the village, and just as the demang's heir might succeed him : but no such right of succession was recognised.

Dr. J. Crawfurd, who was resident at Surakarta, in his history of the Indian Archipelago published in 1820 A. D., says that, in whatever country of the Archipelago arbitrary Government then existed, the titles of the prince, of his nobility, and of many of his officers of Government, would be found generally to be purely Hindu. He goes on to say :—"It is among the Javanese properly so-called that the proprietary right of the sovereign in the soil is most unequivocally established. Such is the universality of this principle that I do not believe, in the whole territory of the native princes, there are a hundred acres over which, by the law or customs of the country, any distinct proprietary right could be pointed out independent of the sovereign. There may be here and there a little forbearance from motives of religion ; but a proprietary right in the soil on the part of a subject, it is not going too far to assert, would be unintelligible to the people, so strongly contrasted are their opinions and ours on this point." And again:—"In the highly peopled provinces of Java, where the population begins already to press on **the** good land, the cultivator exercises no right over the soil, and I hardly know any privilege which he possesses in regard to it except the **liberty** of abandoning it."

The only exceptions to the general rule, which excluded the idea of individual right in landed property, are to be found in the mountainous and wooded tracts occupied by the Sundas in **the** west **of the island,** where private property is established and **the holder's** interest is transferable. This right **has doubtless arisen** in these tracts from the necessity **of** offering superior inducements to the reclaimers of such lands to settle **in** those parts, and it may be compared **to the** rights acquired by ryots in **India who, under clearing** grants, felled **the** dense forests of **the Terai tracts.** The right of the cultivator in his "gaga" **lands, mentioned** by Herr Knops, arises in the same manner. **The** cultivator under native rule paid nominally as land-revenue one-fifth of his produce ; but under unscrupulous officials this was often increased to as much as two-fifths, and Raffles found this rate not an uncommon one. This share might be either taken in kind or at a valuation—a practice exactly similar to that prevailing **in** most of the grain-rented districts of the North of India. Crawfurd describes the process thus :—" Suppose the crop of a given quantity of land consists of 60 parts. One-sixth is deducted at once for reaping, which, in almost all cases, goes to the cultivator and his family. Of the remaining 50 parts, two go to the village priest, after which the remainder is divided into equal parts between the cultivator and the sovereign. The shares of the parties are therefore as follows :—

Cultivator's share	... 34	parts.
Priest ...	... 2	,,
Sovereign ...	... 24	,,
Total	... 60	,,

" One-fifth of the sovereign's share has been occasionally paid as commission for collection. This would reduce the sovereign's actual share to one-third of the gross produce of rice-lands." In addition to this fifth of the produce the officials representing the sovereign could, if they wished it, take the whole produce of the cultivator at the harvest price. The main checks upon the extortionate use of this power were the difficulty of getting rid of the produce and desertion of the villages.

In practice this power was not in the old days abused to any great extent, the wholesome check of emigration restraining the chiefs from going too far. In Java, too, as in India, the power of "adat" (usage), a word clearly introduced by Mahomedans, is great, and high and low obey it. A small ground-rent for houses was also payable by the cultivators, and in many districts a capitation-tax was levied. Then there were contributions at births and marriages in the chief's family, and contributions for charitable and religious objects. The roads, dams and irrigation channels had to be maintained, and the maintenance came out of the pockets of the cultivators. Anglo-Indian officials in the North of India will recognise some of these imposts under the names of "parjot," "marwanah," &c. Besides the land-revenue and other dues the cultivator is bound to render to the sovereign or his representatives one day out of every five of his labour. In 1879, 2,030,136 persons in the island were subject to the corvée, each person being liable for 52 days' labour in the year. In the same year the total population was put at—

Europeans	...	...	29,998
Chinese	...	...	200,303
Arabs	...	...	9,610
Natives	...	...	18,824,574
Others	...	...	3,344
		Total	19,067,829

so that roughly one out of every nine persons is bound to render this service, and there is no doubt whatever that this obligation is much abused up to the present day. Every underling, however low, who can represent himself, truly or not, as the servant of the official, lords it in the village and makes the first cultivator he catches work for him. So also all officials—high and low—passing through the villages, consider themselves entitled to free supplies. These two customs, which almost exactly find their counterparts in the Indian "begari" and "rassad," form the two main counts upon which "Max Havelaar" arraigns the Dutch Government in the powerful indictment which, under the guise of a novel, he brought against his late masters in 1868 A. D. He shows how, up to the present day, the customs which may have had their origin in unobjectionable feudal services, often in the hands of exacting native officials become terrible instruments of oppression, and how the Dutch, while they issue voluminous philanthropic instructions to their officers, in which the protection of the natives figures as one of their first duties, nevertheless shut their eyes to the tyranny which in some regencies is practised with impunity, the general desire being that things may go easily, that there may be no open scandals, and that high native officials, through whom the

Javans are ruled, may be conciliated. It is quite certain that in India abuses under the guise of rassad (supplies) and begari (unpaid labour) are not so flagrant as in Java ; but that they exist every European official will admit, and it is our bounden duty to persistently discourage these practices and protect our native fellow-subjects from themselves.

The system of administration in Java under the native sovereigns was almost identical with that of Akbar in India. We have, under different titles, the same very complete division of the country into provinces, districts, sub-districts and villages. The headmen of the villages were, as in India, chosen by the villagers themselves. The rulers of the sub-districts, districts and provinces, were appointed, and all held office at the pleasure of those who nominated them. With their duties as revenue collectors they combined the offices of criminal and civil judges, being assisted by the Mussulman law officer and a legal counsellor, who was the expounder of local customs which regulated much the dispensing of justice. The parallel between the Javan and Indian system is curiously exact.

When the Dutch had made good their footing in the island they made no attempt to undertake its government. So far as the natives were concerned, they left them and their management entirely to **their** native rulers. Their policy was entirely commercial **and** avowedly selfish. They insisted on certain articles of commerce being kept close monopolies for themselves; they demanded from each district a forced **contingent** of rice, leaving the tumangungs **(or** regents) to **levy it from** the villages in **what** manner they pleased; they compelled the regents to supply whatever labour they required for their public works, and after they had started the coffee plantations, they required the regents to see **that every** cultivator planted, nurtured and plucked a **certain** number of coffee trees; they required that the services of 32,000 families should be placed at their disposal for the felling of timber in the Government forests; and in other ways they endeavoured to **bleed the country for their own benefit,** without attempting to give it anything in return. During this period, therefore, the unhappy country had not only to endure the ills which were indigenous, but it had, in addition, to suffer the oppression consequent on the presence of a foreign power, which insisted on the native rulers extorting produce and forced services from the people for their white masters as well as for themselves. But this **endeavour** on the part of the Dutch to work **the** so-called colony **for** the benefit of the mother-country **by** such a clumsy **and** narrow system, was a disastrous failure. In order to keep up the price **of the** monopoly products they actually often destroyed a large quantity of them; timber accumulated to such an extent that **it rotted** at the depôts; the deficits every **year** became more and more serious, **and** long before the English took possession, the island had ceased **to be of** any commercial advantage to Holland.

Sir Stamford Raffles had **not been long in** Java before he determined **on** a complete change of system. The Dutch monopolies were abandoned, freedom of cultivation was established, **the forced** deliveries **of rice were** stopped, **all tolls on inland** trade were abolished, and taxes on coasting trade removed, the port dues were equalised and their collection taken out of the hands of the Chinese. The salt farms were resumed and administered direct, and the "blandongs" (the system under which the teak forests were worked) were abolished, **a** certain area being reserved to be worked by paid labour, and the rest thrown open to private enterprise. But **the** greatest relief to the people was given in the abolition of all forced services. The coffee plantations were no longer managed as Government properties by compulsory labour. The cultivators were left to keep them up or not, just as they pleased, the Government undertaking to purchase all coffee which the growers could not dispose of in the open market at a rate double that which was paid by the Dutch. The villages were held bound, as heretofore, to furnish their quota of men for works on the roads and other public works; but all this labour was now to be paid for at the regular market rate. In order to provide revenue wherewith to administer the country, Raffles commuted all the imposts on the cultivators into one fixed tax, namely, two-fifths (instead of one-fifth) of the produce; but he took this land-revenue from the first crop only, and allowed the second crop to be cut clear of any tax whatever. Fruit trees and gardens were left free. The cultivator henceforward was to know exactly what would be demanded of him, and would be called upon to make no other contributions either in kind, in money, or in labour.

Raffles then proceeded to reform the land-tenures by excluding, as much as possible, the higher class of natives from any connection with the soil, by leasing the lands direct to the cultivator. During the Dutch rule the native regents would farm out the land-revenues to demangs, and the demangs would sub-let to bukals. Raffles forbad such leases, and reduced the regents and their subordinates to mere collectors of revenue. Village rent-rolls were prepared, and the native collectors had to collect and account in accordance with these. The cultivators were given leases for three years, and it was clearly the intention of Raffles to introduce the ryotwari system of India, and to make the cultivators practically proprietors of their lands. To compensate native officials for their loss of income under these changes, Raffles provided them with handsome salaries and maintained their rank. He also, while he checked their interference in revenue matters, increased their dignity and usefulness by making them act as his police, giving them small correctional powers within their districts : and this is one of the few reforms carried out by Raffles, which were maintained by the Dutch when they resumed possession of the country in 1815 A.D. Torture and mutilation were abolished, and compounding for crime was disallowed ; courts of law were established, and an endeavour was made to secure the benefit of their own laws to the Javans, even in criminal cases, save in cases of murder. The revenue and judicial instructions issued by Sir Stamford to his officers read very like those that might have been issued forty or fifty years ago to the commission of a newly-acquired province in India. That the reforms contemplated and mostly carried out were conceived in a nobly generous spirit and elaborated in a very masterly manner, must be admitted even by the Dutch; but viewing them by the light of our subsequent experience in India, we must hesitate to pronounce some of them to have been either good for the people whom it was Raffles's earnest desire to benefit, or advantageous for the Government.

It was Raffles's intention, as soon as his temporary settlement had expired, to confer on the cultivators the full proprietary right in their holdings, involving the terribly doubtful privilege of alienating their fields and the disastrous liability to be sold up, either by their civil creditors or by the revenue authorities, for default. By the return of the island to Dutch rule the Javans have escaped that fatal gift of absolute proprietary right which has been the ruin of so many tens of thousands of our peasantry in India, and with which, while striving to bless, we have so effectually cursed the soil of

India. It is not too much to say that the loss of all the many benefits which undoubtedly would have been conferred on Java by the substitution of English for Dutch rule, is not too high a price to have paid for escape from the many evils of unrestrained power to alienate landed property. Under their present Government the Javans, according to our English ideas, ought to be the most miserable people. That they are not so, but that, on the contrary, they are the most prosperous of Oriental peasantry, is mainly due to one cause— the inability of the Javan to raise one single florin on the security of his fields, and the protection thus enjoyed by him against the money-lender and against himself. Nature is bountiful in Java, and undoubtedly the abundant fertility of the soil enables the Javan to stand up under many ills to which he is subject; but were her fecundity doubled, were she to pour her gifts as from a cornucopia into his lap, nothing would ultimately save him from the money-lender and from consequent eviction from his fields and his home if he were able to pledge the one or the other as security for an advance.

Herr Mummtingle, one of the Dutch Commissioners whom Raffles consulted in considering the question whether such radical reforms could, politically viewed, be safely carried out in such a conservative country as Java, remarked that the maintenance of the nobles' rank and titles, the attention to their dignity in conferring upon them police jurisdiction and petty magisterial power, the grant of high salaries, and the relief from produce deliveries and money contributions, ought and probably would be considered a sufficient compensation for their loss of profits, but he prophetically added that "the breath of opinion might dissolve even the British power in India," and he counselled caution and a gradual introduction of the system. He also displayed his shrewdness in saying that no order of abolition would suffice to abolish the custom of feudal services being rendered to those to whom they had hitherto been given. The force of "adat" would be too strong even for the British Government. Herr Mummtingle doubtless hit the blot in Raffles' reforms—a blot which has disfigured only too many a page of English administration of Oriental countries. A want of true appreciation of native ideas and incorrect valuation of Oriental methods has always betrayed us into imposing on our fellow-subjects in the East, without tact and without preparation, principles and measures which, however good in themselves, are unintelligible and therefore unwelcome to those whom we wish to benefit. We are so eager to fight abuses and set wrong right that we cannot wait to see whether even in the abuse there may not be latent some principle which, if rightly applied, will enable us to reform instead of eradicate, shape instead of destroy. The Dutch before the time of Raffles, and almost equally so up to the present day, went much too far in the opposite direction. As Sir Stamford says of them:— "They had little other connection with their best subjects—the cultivators of the soil—than in calling upon them from time to time for arbitrary and oppressive contributions and services; and, for the rest, they gave them up to be vassals to the various intermediate authorities, the regents, demangs and other native officers "— a selfish, narrow, iniquitous and withal a suicidal policy. But it at least escaped the evils attendant on the sudden introduction of methods of government necessarily distasteful to the former holders of power and at the same time uncongenial to the people and opposed to their traditional notions of right. Could Sir Stamford Raffles have stopped short of the introduction of the new principle of proprietary right, with its corollaries of power of transfer and mortgage, had he seen his way clear to utilising the labour rent by regulating, instead of abolishing, that much-abused system, and had he thus been able to avoid increasing the share of the produce demandable by the Government, his reforms would have had a better chance of furthering the true interests of the Javan.

The three years of the British administration of the island, however, were not wasted. When the Dutch re-occupied their old possession and found it swept and garnished, they did not proceed to call in the proverbial seven spirits worse than themselves. On the contrary, they began by announcing that they would abolish monopolies of production and allow freedom of cultivation. Further, finding that Singapore, a free port at their very gates, was taking away even such little trade as they already enjoyed, they made a virtue of necessity and largely modified their different duties. But the greatest permanent gains which the Javans obtained from Raffles' rule were the admirable police system and the establishment of courts of justice, both of which reforms were maintained by the Dutch, the former in its entirety and the latter with some modifications. They, however, swept away with decision the ryotwari system, together with the right to sell and be sold up, and reverted, to the great relief of all concerned, to the old village system under which each cottier was allotted at the beginning of the year his parcel of rice-fields, subject to the payment of the grain-revenue. It is asserted by the Dutch (and all who know the manner in which unfamiliar measures are received in India can well believe it) that, in spite of Raffles' endeavour to bestow separate holdings on the cultivators, the Javans continued under the English to manage their affairs in their own way and to cultivate under the annual allotment system as heretofore. The Dutch, however, kept a grip on the land-revenue, which Raffles had for the first time, since Java was occupied by Europeans, brought into the Government treasury. They reduced it from two-fifths to one-fifth of the produce, and, to compensate themselves for the surrender of the extra one-fifth taken by the English, they re-imposed the old labour rent, reducing it from one-fifth of the cultivation labour to one day in seven.

V.

The financial result of Raffles' schemes had been most marked, the revenue rising from $3\frac{1}{2}$ millions of florins in 1810 to $7\frac{1}{2}$ millions in 1814, and the Dutch maintaining the same system were able to continually increase this sum until it reached 24 millions of florins in 1830 A. D. This revenue was, however, only obtained by very severe taxation, and the country could not have gone on yielding this amount. The Government had been engaged for some years in a war with the two native principalities—Surakarta and Jokyokarta—and, in spite of the increasing revenue, deficits were year by year becoming more and more alarming, and Java bid fair to again land Holland in heavy debt. From these difficulties the Dutch were delivered by General Vander Bosch, in 1832 A. D., who initiated what is known as the "culture system." Under this scheme the revenue rose in twenty-five years from 2 millions sterling to $9\frac{1}{2}$ millions sterling annually. The Government with this fine revenue was able during the same twenty-five years to pay off the old Java debt, to raise its unproductive expenditure to 3 millions sterling and its reproductive **expenditure** more than **2 millions,** while the **trade** statistics showed **that imports** had jumped from 2 millions to **5 millions and** exports from 2 millions to 8½ mill**ions. Population rose** during the same period **from 6 millions to 12** millions, and it is calculated that at the present time the population touches 20 millions.

Under the culture system **the** Government **may be** said to have become **farmers** on a gigantic scale. Recognising **the fact** that the soil of **Java** was eminently suitable to the growth of certain valuable products, **such as** sugar, tea, tobacco, coffee, cinnamon, **pepper,** indigo and cochineal, while the native, left to himself, would never exert himself to raise these crops, **the Government** determined in its capacity **of owner of the land to declare that** in the villages **selected** as **suitable at least one-**fifth of the area should be sown with the **crop** prescribed. If the crop was one such as sugar, requiring manufacture on the spot, **a** contractor was placed in the village or group of villages to whom the villagers **were bound** to deliver all the **raw produce as cut,** receiving a fixed price **for** the same. The contractor, who had received **large** advances from the Government to enable him to set **up** the necessary machinery, on his part was bound to deliver a certain quantity of the **manufactured article to the** Government, again, at a fixed price. The result has been enormous profit to the Government, very considerable gain to the contractor, and, the advocates of the system say, great pecuniary advantages to the villagers. Now, when it is considered that not only has the Government, the contractor and the grower **to get their profit** (and it is asserted large profit) out of the article, but the officials—European and native—also receive a handsome percentage on the result in order to interest them in the success of the factory, a sceptic may be led to inquire at what point in the process is the marvel worked which gives such a satisfactory result. It is admitted that private planters, renting land from Government and paying for their labour, are unable to achieve such startling success. The advocates of the culture system say that this arises from the want " of official support among a native population who require authoritative explanation and persuasion to secure continued application of new ideas even for their own good."

Those who are acquainted with Oriental populations will admit that there is some truth in this remark, but the explanation would probably be more correct if **for** " official support" were substituted "official pressure." There can be but little doubt that the factor which determines the profits of the contractor and of the Government is the price **which is** paid for the raw produce to the cultivator. If that is high the profits of the other parties to the bargain will be low: if it is low the superior partners will reap the advantage. Where **the** cultivator **grows** a crop **by** order and receives a price for his produce fixed by him who makes him sow, there is, it need not be said, a terrible temptation to the **latter to make** the most of his opportunity. In **India we are** familiar with this problem in the indigo culture. When indigo commanded a very high price in the market, the planter could afford to give the cultivator compelled by him to sow the plant a fair **price ;** now that indigo **has fallen in value,** the only way to secure good pecuniary **results** is to give such a reduced price for the raw material as barely enables the cultivator to subsist. **Doubtless a** Government, strong to resist temptation, and vigilant in seeing that its paper orders are obeyed, could, when high prices rule, secure to the cultivator a fair price for his produce, and at the same time reap large profits ; but in these days, when such products as sugar and indigo are at such low quotations, it is impossible that under the Javan system large Government profits can be compatible with fair treatment of the cultivator.

This is what Max Havelaar says on this subject, and it is worth quoting at length, as it is the evidence of a Dutchman who had seventeen years of experience of official life in Java:—" The Javan is by nature a husbandman; **the** ground whereon he is born, which gives **mu**ch for little labour, allures him to agricultural work, and, above all things, he devotes his whole heart to the cultivating of his rice-fields. The cultivation of rice **is, in Java, what the** vintage is **in** the Rhine provinces and in the south **of** France. But there came foreigners from the West who made themselves masters of the country. They wished to profit by the fertility of the soil, and ordered the **native** to devote a part of his time and labour **to the cultivation of other things,** which should produce higher profits **in** the markets of Europe. To persuade the lower orders to do **so, they** only had to follow a very simple policy. The Javan obeys his chief: to **win** the chiefs it was only necessary to give them a part of the gains, and success was complete. To be convinced of the success of that policy, we need only consider the immense quantity of Javanese products sold in Holland : and we shall also be convinced of its injustice, for if anybody should ask if the husbandman gets a reward in proportion to that quantity, then I must give a negative answer. **The Government compels him to cultivate certain products** on his ground : it punishes him if he sells what he has produced to any purchaser but itself, and it fixes the price actually paid. The **expenses** of transport to Europe through a privileged trading company are high : the money paid to the chiefs for encouragement increases the prime cost ; and because the entire trade must produce profit, that profit cannot be got in any other way than by paying the Javan just enough to keep him from starving."

This criticism of the culture system was written in **1868 A. D., and no answer to it** has been given officially or unofficially. The Dutch Government gets a clean profit of five millions sterling, and this is a very solid reason for silence. The **average** annual produce of the Government **coffee** plantations for the ten years ending in **1878 A. D.** was 52,000 tons, while the sugar plantations yielded 207,000 tons. The Government of India is not inexperienced in the culture system. It raises its opium revenue by a system identical with that of Java, save in the all-important point that the opium cultivators compete with one another for permission to sow the poppy, while in Java they are compelled to sow the crop named by the contractor-controller. In India also there is no contractor in the business. The factories are managed direct by the Opium Department. Should the demand for opium in China cease, **as seems** not improbable, it might perhaps be possible for the Indian Government to declare tobacco a monopoly, and work its cultivation on the culture system. Indian tobacco is fast finding a European market.

An ingenious device for increasing the **Government** profit was devised by General Vander **Bosch at the** same time as he initiated the culture system. An enormous amount of copper coinage was manufactured in Holland, the intrinsic value being rather less than half the nominal value. This coinage **was** made a legal tender, and the cultivator was paid for his produce in this **copper coin.** Thus, as Mr. Money in his work *Java ; or, How to Manage a Colony,* naïvely remarks :—" The loans, raised in Holland to start the system, produced an effect in Java equal to double their amount."

But when all is said against the culture system, **it** must still be admitted that the cultivating class in Java is distinctly well-to-do. The evidence to be drawn from a personal view of the rural population in their prosperous villages is decisive on this point; and the only conclusion to which we can come is that **the extraordinary fertility of** the soil and the entire absence of the landlord and middleman, enable the Javan peasant to bear up and **even** thrive under a system which violates in many ways our Western principles of justice and fair dealing, and which, unless it is most vigilantly supervised and directed, is capable **of working ruin to the one** who is unable to raise his voice on the **subject.** Crawfurd, speaking of the period when the English had just occupied the country, gives similar testimony to the condition of the people and comes to a like conclusion. He says "that **the habitation of the Javanese peasant is neater,** his clothing and food better, and his modes **of** husbandry more perfect is admitted by all who **have** had an opportunity of instituting a fair comparison between the Hindus and the Javanese;" while, speaking of the exactions levied upon the Javanese, he asks " what but the extraordinary productiveness of the soil and the benignity of the climate, with the peculiar relation of the land to the people, could render such enormous imposts tolerable and present to us, notwithstanding such disadvantages, the extraordinary spectacle of a rich husbandry under such privations as those of the Javanese cultivator."

There is a limit, however, even to the yield of a country such as Java, and when we reflect that the population has quadrupled itself in the island within the past seventy years, and now presses with an incidence of 400 to the square mile, we feel that it will not be long before the Dutch will be face to face with agricultural difficulties similar to those met with in the most congested parts of India, and that it will then perhaps be impracticable to extend, even if it be not found imperative to contract, the cultivation of crops other than cereals. Deficiency in the food-supply has not been unknown even in Java, and Holland had once to issue an order that "the extension of the so-called European market should no longer be pushed to the extremity of famine."

Again, the Dutch Government must most jealously exclude the landlord and the middleman. If, as it seems is not unlikely to be the case, the independent planter steps into the place of the Government, armed with all its power, but untrammelled by its respect for public opinion, or its desire to do its duty by the native, the great safeguards which at present exist will be removed. It is clear that considerable pressure has been for some time brought to bear upon the Java Government by the unofficial Dutch in the island to withdraw from the culture system in favour of the private speculators, and in 1870 a new law permitted the cession of uncultivated land to Europeans on lease for 85 years. In Batavia, and the other large towns where the European merchants have their houses of business, not unfrequently opinions are expressed adverse to the present administration under which the profits from the culture system are absorbed by the mother-country instead of being spent in Java; and sometimes these opinions are sufficiently unpatriotic to take the form of a wish that the English may, at some time or other, again be masters in Java, in which event, it is predicted, the colony will get fair play. But it is not difficult for those who pursue the subject with such discontented Dutchmen to see that it is not on behalf of the country or of the Javans that they are indignant at the present state of things, but on behalf of themselves. They are pretty well assured that the English, if they ever did re-occupy the country, would abandon at once their position as producers, as militating against the free trade principle, and that the plantations would be handed over to private venture. Then would come the time of the speculator—Dutch, English and Chinese: and from that day forward woe to the unfortunate Javan, who would look back with longing regret to the days when his only master was a Government, selfish doubtless in its aims, but still discreet in the exercise of its power.

VI.

Java and Madura are now divided into twenty-five residencies, which comprise seventy-eight regencies, each of which latter divisions is ruled by a native regent, "assisted" by an assistant resident, who has as his lieutenant in his work a "controller." At the head-quarters of each residency is the resident, with powers of supervision over the officers in charge of the regencies. The work of administration is supposed to be done by the native regent, and all orders to the people are issued through him. The actual rulers are of course the Dutch; but it is their settled policy to carry, if possible, the native upper classes with them in their administration, and they endeavour to secure this object, even at the risk of much inconvenience and ineffectual government, which but too often results from this dual rule. The regency is again divided into small districts, each under the immediate orders of a " Wedana," who is, like the regent, a native of high family, with "mantries" under him. These "mantries," who are officials corresponding to the petty officers of police and the irrepressible chuprassies of India, are the relations generally of the regent and the Wedanas. A regency thus is usually packed full of the regent's own people. How difficult therefore Max Havelaar found it to convict a regent of oppression and abuses may easily be understood. This impunity for native wrong-doers in high places is a necessary consequence of the Dutch policy. In each village there is a headman, who is elected by the villagers. This man collects the land tax, allots the rice-fields, keeps the roster of men to work on the plantation or the roads, sees to the supply of gratuitous provisions for the mantries and others, and tells off the villagers as watchmen in their turn. He settles small disputes, and being chosen by the people he is trusted by them and is really a protection to them.

The work of governing this patient people is done smoothly—too smoothly. Where the surface is so unrippled, one may suspect strong currents underneath, and it is one of Max Havelaar's charges that it is well understood in Java all round that reports are usually to have *couleur de rose*. The Government of Dutch " India," he says, " likes to write home to its masters in the mother-country that all goes on satisfactorily. The residents like to announce this to the Government. The assistant residents, who receive themselves from their controllers nothing but favourable accounts, send again, in their turn, no disagreeable tidings to the residents. From all this there arises in the official written accounts of these matters an artificial optimism, contradictory not only to the truth, but also to the real opinion of these optimists themselves." How great the undercurrents may be sometimes may be judged from the fact that in April, 1889, no less than a hundred natives of Bantam (Max Havelaar's district) were lying under sentence of death for insurrection.

The principle upon which the courts of justice are based is the conferment of very limited powers indeed on both European and native officers sitting alone, even the resident himself being unable to inflict a severer punishment than ten days' imprisonment, while the Joint Court, called the " Landraad," in which the resident and regent with one other native of high rank sit together, can inflict the penalty of death subject to confirmation of the Supreme Government at Batavia. No Europeans, however, are subject to any other than purely Dutch courts. The Landraad is the principal civil as well as criminal court for natives, the resident, regent and Wedana exercising petty civil jurisdiction when sitting alone. Great consideration is shown for the sensibilities of natives of high rank, even when charged with serious offences, and arrests of such persons are not made except under high authority. The Dutch have avoided one of our difficulties in absolutely declining to sanction anything in the shape of a native bar. The vakil is not, and no one is allowed to plead for another who is not his personal friend. For this mercy the Javan may be thankful that the English rule did not continue. Litigation receives therefore no unhealthy stimulus. Perhaps some might be inclined to think that the criminal courts are unduly idle, for the Landraads are said to sit not oftener than thirty days in the year. Probably a large amount of crime never comes to light at all.

The dual system, which pervades all the Dutch institutions in Java, holds good in the army also. Each regiment is composed both of Europeans and natives, the former taking the flank companies, the latter the centre, and the plan is said to work extremely well. There are also a number of negroes in the ranks, and the Government takes Europeans of all kinds as recruits for its white army. After the Crimean War the Foreign Legion largely found service in Java. All Dutchmen in the island are liable to military service; but in ordinary times their obligations only extend to putting in a certain number of drills every year. These are rigorously exacted, and there is therefore, besides the 35,000 regular troops, a large body of this militia on which to fall back upon in time of need. As there is no landed aristocracy and the natives of position mostly hold lucrative appointments under Government, and as an Arms Act is strictly enforced among the lower orders, the Dutch are not likely to be annoyed with insurrections. Their only troublesome neighbours are the two Sultans of Surakarta and Jokyokarta; but these potentates are only allowed to keep a small body of troops, and they are watched by a force at Magellang, on the northern border of these Principalities. The Sultans receive large money allowances from the Dutch and also have private domains; but they are, it seems, well nigh powerless for mischief. In the Indian Netherlands the Dutch have, of course, a standing trouble in Achin, at the N.-W. of Sumatra. For the past fifteen years the Achinese have kept the Dutch at bay, and the latter's rule in this part of Sumatra is limited to the range of their guns from the fort. The whole of Java's fine surplus revenue is swallowed up in this weary struggle, and Holland no longer credits the Home treasury, as she was wont, with three or four millions annually. She would gladly hand over to England Sumatra, and thus get honourably quit of her unprofitable possession.

From the slight sketch of Java and its institutions which has been given it will have been seen how different are the methods of government adopted by Holland and England in their administration of their Oriental possessions. We strive our very best to rule India in the interest of the native population. The Dutch do not profess to study the well-being of their Javan subjects, save as an object secondary to their own advantage. England expends the whole of her enormous revenue in India and sends not a rupee westwards, save for goods purchased, while Holland receives ordinarily from Java, as pure tribute, more than one-third of her colony's income. We lay ourselves out to give every Indian who cares to come forward for it what is practically a free education right up to the Universities which we have established, and still continue to establish, all over India: Holland of set purpose keeps its Eastern subjects as stupid and ignorant as is possible. We are scrupulously exact in all our dealings with the natives, insisting on a full wage being paid for all work done, and checking, by all the means in our power, the tendency on the part of all natives in authority to compel labour, while the Dutch have no hesitation in utilising to the full this tendency and practically draw from this source a large portion of their revenue. The English protect all rights in land, however shadowy they may be, and confer others : the Dutch admit no such rights and studiously avoid the introduction of the proprietary principle. We persist in impressing on the native mind that the Western and the Oriental, the heir of Europe's civilisation and successor to Eastern conservatism, are all equal and equally fitted for, and capable of, understanding and of profiting by those social institutions and forms of government to which we ourselves are so attached : the Dutch frankly deny the equality and ridicule the notion that all the world should be ruled on the same principle.

To the Anglo-Indian visiting Java and viewing these great differences it is somewhat humiliating to feel that the Dutch have most unquestionably, in one point at any rate, succeeded where we have partially failed. Conscious of the absolutely upright intentions of his own Government, and convinced that it is the first wish of every English official connected with the administration that all classes should share in the blessings which should flow from its benevolent measures, he is startled to find the great mass of agriculturists in Java manifestly in a far better material condition than our own ryots. This is unquestionably the case, and the fact undoubtedly proves that our treatment of the great questions relating to land-tenures, which a hundred years ago were partly similar to those which have from time to time arisen in Java, have not been dealt with in the manner best calculated to secure the happiness of the people. The denationalisation of the land, which from the time of Lord Cornwallis till the present day has been more and more completely effected, has resulted in the aggrandisement of a class of wealthy landlords and middlemen at the expense of the cultivator of the soil, and we have surrendered that splendid position as owners of the land which enables the Dutch to appropriate for State purposes the whole rental of the country and to ensure that that rental shall always be so moderate in amount as to enable the peasant to pass his days in comfort and without care. Doubtless Holland would do well to treat her rich dependency in a more generous, more unselfish spirit, and in many points she could undoubtedly take lessons from England : but the impartial student of the economics of the Eastern possessions of the two countries will certainly come also to the conclusion that India has much to learn from Java.

APPENDIX.

THE STUPA OF BORO BODHO.

The devout Buddhist who erected the Great Stupa of Boro Bodho in Java in honour of the Teacher must have been as keenly appreciative of the loveliness of nature as of the beauty of holiness. Few more lovely spots in the beautiful isle of Java can exist than that plateau which lies to the south of the Sendoro range, a range which, near Boro Bodho, might fitly be called a sierra, so rugged and sharp in outline are the jagged peaks which rise up into the sky from the main ridge of hills. On this plateau, from which rise the giant volcanoes Merbabu and Merapi and other minor cones right and left as the traveller journeys from Jokyokarta to Magellang, is the residency of Kedu, one of the most interesting, most beautiful and most fertile tracts in the whole island. The river Progo traverses the plateau from north to south and approaches within a couple of miles the range of rocky hills under which has been built the Great Stupa.

The Stupa itself is built on a small natural hill about two hundred feet high, and, as the traveller ascends this, he recognises what an admirable site was chosen for such an edifice. At his feet lies a plain of unexampled richness, broken here and there by small hamlets embowered in foliage and by other smaller hills such as that on which he stands. Behind him at a little distance flows the Progo, sometimes symbolising in its violence the uncontrolled passions of him who has not found the Path, but now flowing with the peacefulness of a soul at rest; while in front rise the eternal hills, dead silent in their quietness and strength, a fit panorama for the devout one whose method is self-control and annihilation of desire, and whose aim is freedom from all delusion and defilement, freedom from all sense of his surroundings, freedom from all sin and sorrow and the attainment of " Nirvana," that Rest which cannot be shaken, that Peace which can never be lost.

The Stupa occupies the upper part of the hill, the base of the structure being carried along the sides of the mound about half-way up the ascent, while the topmost cupola rests on the summit of the natural hill. The building, which is pyramidal in form, has thus the hill itself for its support throughout, the massive galleries and terraces, which rise from the base to the summit, having been built on corresponding stages cut in the sides of the slopes. The whole is built of the volcanic stone which lies in great profusion all over this part of the plateau, and which is evidently the result of some mighty eruption of Mount Merapi in ages past. It is a stone which lends itself to sculpture and which enables the smallest details to be worked out, while its power of resistance to sun and rain, even though these be tropical in their destructive strength, is evidenced by the wonderful state of preservation in which most of the work still exists.

The whole is put together without any mortar or cement of any kind, the stones, which are very large, being exceedingly cleanly chiselled and accurately fitted one into the other. The edifice thus gains an elasticity which, combined with the pyramidal form of construction, has doubtless secured it against destruction or excessive damage by earthquakes which are both frequent and severe in Java.

At its base the building, as it now exists, is a square, each side being 370 feet in length. At a distance, however, of 40 feet from each corner the line is admirably broken by the structure being projected forward about eight feet, and after another run of frontage for 60 feet from each corner of this projection the building again advances eight feet. This variation, in what would otherwise have been a somewhat monotonous frontage, is a most artistic device and proclaims the architect a master. The first terrace to which we ascend is about eight feet above the ground and is quite plain, without any ornamentation, except some lions posted on its edge. A discovery has quite lately been made, since the publication of M. Leeman's splendid monograph, that this first terrace never formed part of the original building, but was undoubtedly added by some one who thought to mend, but very nearly succeeded in marring, the beauty of the pile. This plinth has actually been piled up against what was originally the outermost wall of the Stupa, thus completely hiding from view the beautiful bas-reliefs which adorned that wall and which now lie buried beneath the mass of masonry which forms this superfluous terrace. It is the intention of the Dutch to remove this addition to the Stupa as designed by the Buddhist architect, obtain drawings of the sculptured walls now buried and then replace it, stone by stone, so that the building many remain just as found by them. They would be fully justified in removing it permanently. When it is gone, the length of each side of the building will be reduced to 330 feet, the false terrace being 20 feet in width.

The total height from the base of the original structure to the top of the central cupola is about 130 feet. The grand pile rises by a series of galleries and terraces (four of the former and three of the latter) which run round the entire building, the whole leading up to a massively built dagaba in which sits the principal Buddha, in whose honour the Stupa was erected.

Four staircases, one in the centre of each face of the building, give access from below to this shrine, and at the same time enable the pilgrim to reach the galleries which, as he ascends the steps, he finds to the right and left. Each of these galleries is sunk between the parapet (about seven feet high) on the outer side and the wall of the gallery next above, so that, though the whole building were crowded with people, all would appear quiet and solitary from outside.

To the pilgrim passing through these galleries is displayed a superb series of sculptured stories, all in bas-relief, carved in panels on the walls on either side. These beautiful entablatures originally numbered no less than 1,554, of which about 1,350 still exist—all in excellent preservation. The lowest gallery alone contains 346 bas-reliefs, measuring each 10 by 3, besides

496 others, each measuring 3 by 3 or 3 by 2. The second gallery contains 332 such sculptures, the third gallery 162 and the fourth 212. The whole show by their style that they must have been executed by artists who had not long left India, so clearly Indian in character are both the design and execution. The tale told in the lowest gallery, where the greatest number of panels are crowded on to the walls, is, it would seem, the life of the great Teacher, from the time when his father King Saddhodana received the congratulations of the neighbouring princes on the expected birth of his son until the enlightened one passed away, impressing on the members of his order the efficacy of the Law. The upper galleries appear to be allegorical, illustrating the doctrine of Buddha, points of the Law and the power of faith. But much which has been written by Wilson on this subject in Leeman's description of the sculptures appears to be conjectural, and it is not at all certain that we have yet got the clue to this marvellous series of bas-reliefs.

On the parapets of the walls which enclose these galleries there are ranged a large number of life-size Buddhas, each seated under a canopy. They number no less than 336 in all, 88 occupying the lowest rampart, 72 the next,

64 the third, 64 the fourth, and 48 the fifth. The figures are admirably carved, the face having that serene expression of perfect rest and content which is the unvarying characteristic of the Buddha.

Above these again, ranged on three circular terraces around the central cupola, are 72 more Buddhas, also of life-size, seated within chaityas constructed in the form of a bell, the side of the bell being made of open stone-work, the perforations admitting light and allowing the faithful to view the seated saint.

The presence of these Buddhas is a conclusive proof that it was the Northern Buddhist Church the doctrine and ritual of which were observed in Java. That church recognised five principal Manushi or human Buddhas: (1) Krakuchanda, (2) Ranakamund, (3) Kasyapa, (4) Gautama, (5) Maitreya. The three first are supposed to have entered the world in the ages before Gautama (he of the Sakya family), who is the only historical Buddha and the founder of the Buddhist religion. The fifth, Maitreya, the Buddha of loving kindness, has not yet appeared, but is looked for 5,000 years after Gautama.

The heavenly counterparts of these five Buddhas, called the Dhyani Buddhas, are : (1) Vairochana, (2) Akshobhya, (3) Ratna-sambhava, (4) Amitabha, (5) Amogasiddha. These inhabit the ethereal mansions, free from the debasing conditions of this material life, while the earthly and mortal (Manushi) Buddhas appear incarnate on the earth. They are the five Dhyani or heavenly Buddhas whose statues to the number of 408 have their places, as **mentioned** above, on the galleries **and** terraces of the Great Stupa of **Boro** Bodho.

Vairochana occupies the three highest circular terraces. He is **represented with** the fingers in the attitude of laying **down the** heads of the " Four Truths" and of the "Noble Eight-fold Path," in the fourth stage of which the seeker after holiness becomes free from all sin and only experiences pure desires for himself, tender pity, and **exalted spiritual love for** others. This stage in the Path reached, he has attained Nirvana.

Akshobhya, who is always represented with his hand resting palm downwards on his knee, occupies the four lower galleries, looking to **the** east, where is his own special Paradise. **In** this attitude is also found the Buddha **in the** central cupola which crowns the Stupa.

Ratna-sambhava, whose hand **is always** on **his knee with** the palm upwards, as if asking for alms, holds his place on the four lower galleries looking south, the direction of his celestial home.

Amitabha, the heavenly counterpart of Gautama, has his hands crossed on his lap, the palms upward, in the attitude of meditation. He is found on the four galleries looking west, the Paradise which he quitted to appear on earth as the " Light of Asia."

Amogasiddha, whose hand is raised in the attitude of blessing, occupies the four lower galleries looking north, the Paradise where he is awaiting his turn to come on earth and bless the world. This Buddha also is found on all four faces of the topmost gallery, just below the terraces occupied by Vairochana, there being a slight difference in the position of the fingers in this representation of him.

The doctrines of the Northern Church were a late development of the Buddhist religion and were, it seems, certainly introduced after the time of Fa Hian, who makes no mention of any such phase. Fa Hian's note therefore that he found no Buddhists in Ye-pho-ti (Java) is corroborated by the fact that Buddhism, whenever it was introduced, was that of the northern branch, not of the southern. Another much later development was the dea of the Sakti or female Buddha, the consort of Buddha in heaven. This degenerate idea did not arise until the simple and pure morality of Gautama's system had been invaded by all kinds of metaphysical refinements, the original teaching of the **master** being lost in a Babel of fanciful discussions tending towards a degraded mysticism. Buddhism adopted this last idea of the Sakti about the twelfth century of our era, and if it is true that on the outside wall of the original lowest gallery we have, in a female figure which continually recurs, the representation of the Sakti, we have the evidence that the Stupa could **not have** been built earlier than that period. That the figure alluded to is that of the Sakti is, however, exceedingly doubtful, and the male figure with which the female is associated is not of the **same** simple and severe **type** as the Buddhas within the galleries. **It is possible** that these figures on the outside wall represent the prince and princess who erected the Stupa. Setting aside the supposition that this figure is that of the Sakti, there is nothing in any one of the other sculptures to lead us to infer that the building was erected at any time other than when the Buddhist religion was comparatively pure and simple. One fact seems clear, namely, that Boro Bodho was built when Buddhism had completely prevailed over Brahmanism, for there is in this building no vestige of the latter religion. In most of the sacred buildings of Java we find traces of the two religions side by side, and even in Mendoet, a temple not three miles from Boro Bodho, while the interior is occupied by Buddha and two Bodhi-satwas, the outside of the building is adorned with bas-reliefs undoubtedly Brahmanical. So frequently do we find this admixture of the two faiths that we should have expected to meet with it in Boro Bodho, but this is not the case: the Stupa is purely Buddhistic throughout.

In the present stage of antiquarian research in Java it is not possible to assign a certain date to the construction of this magnificent Stupa. No certain data have yet been obtained from the buildings themselves. The "Babads," or chronicles of Java, which are all comparatively recent, speak of Boro Bodho as of very ancient date, but they do not assign it to any particular age or particular kingdom. Their evidence is so far valuable that it is shown from them that the Stupa was in existence when they were written: but these Babads themselves are so contradictory, one of the other, that it is impossible to assign certain dates even to them. We must wait patiently for satisfactory testimony as to the age in which, and the circumstances under which, this grand building was conceived and executed, and in the meanwhile we may gaze and **admire** the devotion which could inspire such a poem.

INDEX

Aji Saka, 3, 4, 5.
Augka Wijaya, 10.

Bali, Island of, ii ; **5, 10, 16, 19, 39.**
Banjuwangi, 17.
Bantam, **11, 13,** 74.
Batavia, ii ; 2, **19,** 74.
Boro Bodho, 3, 6, 7, 8, 9.
Boro Bodho, Stupa of, 81.
Bram-Banam, 2, 6.
Bram-Banam, Boundary of, 5.
Burma, 8.

Ceylon, 8.

Dress of the Javans, 25.
Dutch East India Company, **15.**
Dutch in Java, First, **13.**
Dutch wars in Java, 13, 14.

English occupation of Java, 16.

Fa Hian, 4.
Flores, 17.

Galung-gung, 17.
Government of Java, 72.
Grobogan, 17.
Gujerat, 3.

Hong-Kong, i.

Jakatra, 13.
Java, i, ii, iii, iv ; **1, 5,** 6, 7, 8, 9, **10, 11, 13, 14, 16,** 18, 20, 21, 24, 27, 34, 36, 40, 41, 42, 44, 45, 48, 50, 56, 60, 61, 62, 65, 67, 68, 69, 70, 72, 76, 78, 79, 80, 81, 83.
Java, Area of, 16.
Java, Dutch wars in, 13, 14.

INDEX

Java, English occupation of, 16.
Java, First appearance of the Dutch in, 13.
Java, Government of, 72.
Java, Indian Art in, 3.
Java, Land System in, 42.
Java, Marriage Customs in, 35.
Java, Portuguese in, 11.
Java, Products of, 20, 21.
Java, Soil of, 18.
Java, Temperature of, 19.
Java, Volcanoes in, 17.
Java era, Commencement of, 3.
Jokyokarta, 14, 17, 76, 81.

Kedu, 81.
Krakatoa, 17.
Kuda Lalean, 9.

Land System in Java, 42.
Land-tax in Java, 53.
Leemans, C., 8.
Literature of Java, 40.
Lombok, ii ; 17.

Madura, Island of, 5, 13, 39, 72.
Magellang, 76, 81.
Majapahit, 13.
Majapahit, Kingdom of, 10.
Malay, Archipelago, 1.
Manhu Buni, 14.
Marriage Customs in Java, 35.
Matarem, 5, 14.
Mendang Kamulan, 5, 6.
Merapi, 17, 81.
Merbabu, 81.

Nepal, 9.

Pandu Devanatta, 3.
Panji, 9.
Portuguese in Java, 11.
Prabhu Jaya Bhaya, 3, 5.
Products of Java, 20, 21.

INDEX

Progo, 81, 82.

Raden Wijaya, 10.
Raffles, Stamford, 2, 16,   52, 54, 55, 56, 58, 59, 60.
Rasaksas, 3.
Religion of Java, 3.

Saddhodana, 86.
Samarang, 19.
Sawela Chala, 5.
Semeru, 17.
Singapore, ii ; 59.
Soerabia, 19.
Soil of Java, 18.
Sombawa, 17.
Stupa of Boro Bodho, 81.
Sumatra, 5, 10, 15, 17, 76, 77.
Surakarta, 14, 45, 61, 76.
Susuhnan, 14.
Sydney, i.

Teak Forests, 18.
Temperature of Java, 19.
Tibet, 9.
Timor, 17.
Tritesta, 4.

Volcanoes in Java, 17.

www.ingramcontent.com/pod-product-compliance
Lightning Source LLC
Chambersburg PA
CBHW021947160426
43195CB00011B/1265